Kids

A play

John Morgan

Samuel French—London
New York-Toronto-Hollywood

KIDS

The first performance of *Kids* was at Westminster School, London, on February 4th and 5th, 1997. The cast was as follows:

Baby	Leonora Borg
Johnny	Alexie Calvert-Ansari
Sam	Nick Clark
Wendy	Sophie Powell
Ellie	Lucy Priest

Directed by Philip Needham

CHARACTERS

Baby, 6 months old
Johnny, almost 3
Sam, nearly 5
Wendy, 7
Ellie, 9

The action of the play takes place in a playground

Time: the present

PRODUCTION NOTE

This is a play about childhood. The characters are all played by adults dressed in appropriate clothing. The sex of the children is pretty immaterial and the parts can be played by men or women with appropriate changes in name and gender reference.

KIDS

The set is a children's playground. Everything is out of proportion. A giant swing hangs DL. At the back is a climbing frame that extends haphazardly across the stage and at times high up. Its highest point is R. There is a rug CR

As the CURTAIN opens, there is the sound of children playing. The sound fades, to be replaced by a baby crying. A spot lights up the area of the swing

Ellie is standing there with a skipping rope in her hands

Ellie Does a lot of that. The baby. I could strangle him. Sometimes. Most of the time. But when you start, he just looks at you and you could eat him. He loves everybody. He can do amazing things. He can suck his toes. He looks comfortable whichever way up he is. He can fart longer and harder than anyone I know. And it doesn't matter how much he eats, he always manages to sick up more than you give him.

He concentrates hard on everything. When he dribbles, he seems to have worked it out first. He looks so wise and all he can say is "mama" and "dada".

The Lights cross-fade to the general state

Ellie exits R

The Baby is sitting on the rug. He is playing absently with his fingers and making appropriate noises

Johnny and Sam are playing on the frame

Ellie enters R, *punches Johnny in the stomach and pinches Sam. She pushes the Baby over and skips off* L

Johnny (*winded*) With any luck she'll trip over the baby's bottle that he so thoughtfully threw over there.

There is a crash off stage and a scream, followed by a short tantrum and whimpers

Thought so.
Sam Do you think we'll grow into something like that?
Johnny Inevitably.
Sam Christ.

The Baby is lying on his side, in the most peculiar position, gurgling and muttering

Johnny Should someone sit him up?
Sam I don't think he's that bothered. One of the adults might notice eventually.

Wendy enters L *and begins to skip with the rope, chanting mindlessly*

Wendy   Loo, loo, skip to my loo.
                                 Loo, loo, skip to my loo.
                                 Loo, loo, skip to my loo.
                                 Skip to my loo my toilet.
Sam Language is a wonderful thing.
Johnny Can't come soon enough for me. I want to tell 'em all a thing or two.
Sam You'll forget it all when you've got the words to say it.
Johnny Mmmmmm.

Wendy sits the Baby upright and skips again, humming tunelessly. The others watch

Ellie enters L, steals the skipping rope and runs off R

Wendy Bastard.

Wendy pushes the Baby over, slaps Sam, tweaks Johnny's nose and then runs after Ellie

Johnny There goes the future. She's got a hope. Ellie will beat the living shit out of her.

There are violent sounds off and a squeal

What it's like to be right all the time.
Sam That won't last.

Wendy enters with the skipping rope wrapped around her face, sits the Baby up, removes the rope and starts playing with the Baby. It looks painful for the Baby, but he doesn't seem to mind

Johnny She's sitting where he was sick before, isn't she?
Sam Yeah. She'll notice in a minute.
Wendy (*leaping to her feet*) You mucky little pig. Mam!

Wendy exits hurriedly L, feeling her bottom for wetness. Sam and Johnny wander over to play with the Baby

Sam Interesting beast. Look. (*He demonstrates*) If you put your finger in his eye, he closes it.
Johnny So do you. (*He demonstrates*)

Sam pinches him

I see. Early developer.
Sam You wouldn't think he had the IQ of Albert Einstein and Bertrand Russell put together, would you? (*He examines the Baby's ear*)
Johnny Well, we all did once. Soon get it knocked out of us, though. (*He experimentally pushes the Baby like a bobbing toy*)

Sam gets up suddenly

Sam Let's play on the swing.

They take each other's hand and run over. One stands on either side and looks up at it

Johnny It's a long way up.
Sam When we're big enough to reach it, we'll be too old to enjoy it.

They reach up and hang from either side of the swing

Johnny If you help me, I could sit on this.
Sam You'll fall off.
Johnny All you've got to do is give me a leg up. It's easy.
Sam You'll fall off.
Johnny It won't take a moment.
Sam You will. You'll fall off.
Johnny Look. I don't expect you to understand this, but it's
   important.
Sam You'll only fall off.

They stand behind the swing. Johnny inexpertly climbs on Sam so that he can lift himself on to it, standing on his hands, shoulder and head to do so. He lays his chest on the swing. Sam stands back. Johnny falls off

I told you you'd fall off.

Johnny cries

   Sam takes his hand and they exit L

The Lights cross-fade to a spot which lights up the Baby's blanket

Baby It takes a lot longer than nine months. Sometimes there are
   years of courtship and planning, pain and hardship. It's hardly a

"I was just scrubbing the floor and then, whoops, out he popped". The birth hurts and often takes ages. Family income is disrupted, routine is chopped about, relationships have to be renegotiated. It is a messy business having a baby. And it doesn't end there. Years of trauma follow it for everybody concerned. There's the problems of health, education, socialisation. Oh, yes, that's the bugger, socialisation. And the expense. If you worked out what it cost there wouldn't be any more people. Why in God's name do they do it?

And what about me. I was a free spirit. I touched the universe. My mind and soul were unbounded. I knew everything and rejoiced in the wholeness of it. I was at one with creation. Then my parents had to have sex.

You prats! Why couldn't you leave me alone? Why did you have to land me in this heap of dribbling blubber?

The Lights cross-fade to the general state

Ellie and Wendy enter R. Each holds one end of the skipping rope. They wander across to the climbing frame, looking at the Baby

Wendy What do you think he was crying for?
Ellie Probably needs changing. Don't go near him. He's got nits.
Wendy He smells.

They start to swing the rope

Sam enters and hangs from the swing

Ellie We need somebody else to skip. Sammy!
Wendy He's too little. He drops the rope.

Sam comes over, suspiciously. Ellie ties the rope around his neck

Ellie Now stay there. You turn and I'll skip.

Wendy (*defiantly*) My rope!
Ellie (*through her teeth*) You turn!
Wendy (*bravely*) My rope!

Ellie pounces on Wendy and they roll around on the stage. There is no doubt as to the outcome. Ellie beats her into submission

> *Sam wanders off R with the rope around his neck. Wendy pushes over the Baby and runs off L, crying*

Ellie There, there. (*She sits the Baby up and consoles him*)

> *Johnny enters carrying the Baby's bottle as if it were a gun. He shoots things around him*

Johnny Pshoom. Pshoom. Pshoom.
Ellie Bang. Bang.
Johnny Pshoom.
Ellie That a laser gun, Johnny?
Johnny (*looking down at it*) No. 'Sa baby's bottle.
Ellie (*wrinkling up her nose*) Oh, my God. You dirty little animal.

> *She holds her nose theatrically and leaves L*

Johnny sits with the Baby

Johnny You farted, didn't you?
Baby No. I filled my nappy. Best way of getting rid of her. Only one thing worse than being pushed over by Wendy, being sat up again by her.

Johnny plays with the Baby's face

I was just thinking. It is interesting how the space-time continuum is curved. (*He tries to suck his toes and fails. He ends up sucking his thumb*) If you could see far enough you could just about spot the back of your own head; assuming that the speed of light is instantaneous; which, of course, it is, since time is an illusion. If it wasn't for the limitation of these damned senses of ours…

Johnny You worked out all that for yourself, didn't you? (*He peers into the Baby's ear*)

Baby Well, it's obvious, isn't it?

Johnny Used to be. Getting harder now.

Sam wanders in, the skipping rope still around his neck

Ellie and Wendy enter L, *hand in hand*

Sam begins to play with Johnny and the Baby

Wendy What do you suppose they think they're talking about?

Ellie Baby talk. They'll grow out of it.

Johnny I must get up on to that swing. How do you think I can do it?

Baby Remember how to co-operate? You just need the help of those big prats over there.

Wendy and Ellie come over. Each one grabs one end of the rope and they begin to pull. Sam tries to get it off and fails

Ellie Let's skip.

Wendy My rope.

Ellie Should he be turning that colour?

Sam is gasping for breath

Johnny They never listen to me.

Baby They might listen to Sammy, though.

Ellie Gimme.

Wendy No.

There is the sound of the ice-cream van

At once the two girls rush off R, *their argument forgotten*

Johnny Sammy?

Sam (*removing the rope with difficulty and gasping for breath still*) What?

Johnny I really do have to get on that swing.

Sam You'll fall off.

Johnny Just think for a minute. Try and remember. I have to do it. Help me.

Sam You know I can't. I'm too little. You'll fall off.

Johnny I asked the baby. He says we just have to get those two to co-operate.

Sam Fat chance.

The girls return with five ice-creams and hand some over to the Baby and the two boys

The Baby plays with his and begins to cover everything around him with it

What's he doing?

Johnny (*vaguely*) Oh, some experiment with matter conservation. I used to do that. Nearly solved it. Adults kept wiping it off or taking it away before I finished. (*Beat*) I know. Tell them they can have my ice-cream if they help.

Sam You're out of your skull.

Johnny No. Go on.

Sam Johnny says if you help him get on the swing you can have his ice-cream.

Wendy What's wrong with it?

Sam Nothing much. He's just licked it a bit and chewed the end off.

Ellie (*factually*) It's dribbling out at the bottom.

Sam (*decisively*) Well, you'd better say "Yes", then, before it's all gone.

The girls take the ice-cream and exit L

I said you were out of your skull.

Johnny No problem. Watch this. (*He bursts into tears*)

Sam What you doing?
Johnny Stick and carrot, old son, stick and carrot. Threaten to tell
Mam they stole my ice-cream.

The girls enter without the ice-creams

Ellie What's up with 'im?
Sam 'E said you took 'is ice-cream. (*He bursts into tears*) Telling
Mam.
Wendy 'E didn't want it!
Ellie Tell him to shut up or I'll kill him.
Wendy Mam's coming over.
Sam Well, put him on the swing then.
Wendy He'll fall off.
Ellie For God's sake put him on it.

The crying stops at once

(*To* L) Nothing, Mam. No, he's fine. Jus' laughing at the baby,
Mam. Yes, Mam. Honest. No, Mam. Yes, Mam.

*The girls make as if to leave. The crying starts immediately. They
turn*

Wendy Oh, for God's sake.

*Wendy and Ellie go for Johnny, take him to the swing, and lift him
into the seat with difficulty. The crying stops*

Everyone exits but the Baby and Johnny

*The Lights cross-fade to a spot on the swing. Johnny keeps his
balance with some difficulty*

Johnny (*to the audience*) Yes, I know. Some would say brave.
Some would say foolhardy. But the real question is why? Why?
(*He looks down tremulously*) Why does a three-year-old get

himself into this kind of position? I spent all that effort getting up
here… and I can't get down now… (*Worried*) Well, it is important. (*Firmly*) It is important. As time goes on, I forget why; but
I think I can explain.

For a start, it's symbolic. Don't dismiss that; not right away.
Think about the powerful symbols you use every day. Letters of
the alphabet, numbers to count. The Cross. Think about martyrs
as symbols and the way they stretch the imagination and
change the universe. Think about $E=mc^2$ and the atom bomb.
Me getting up here is just as symbolic and just as powerful.

The reality is that when we are born we are neither good nor bad.
We are all endowed with massive intelligent potential, even those
with damage caused through their genes, or physical handicap.
We are all zestful and joyful. We are totally loving and lovable.
Look at the unselfish love that exudes from the littlest of us. We
are all co-operative and able to work together for common ends.
We are all unconditionally powerful. A toddler can look the
Queen right in the eye without flinching and be sick on her dress.
You try doing that.

We lack two things. Physical strength and information.

What happens then? Why, patterns of distress knock a lot of it out
of us. Most of us start life with a damn good thumping in a cold
noisy place. Then starts our socialisation. It is passed down the
line from the adults. Physical, mental and metaphysical bullying
knocks us into conformity. It turns into one great competition in
which the rules are made up as you go along and nobody quite
knows them. What is most astonishing is that we are not all mental
wrecks by the time we get out of our teens. In the process, of
course, we are conditioned to keep it all going. And the reward is
some physical strength, some information, and a lot of misinfor-
mation. The baby says that all infants are born free but that
everywhere adults are in chains.

That is why I am up here. I have striven above my limitations…

And I'm scared stiff … and I want my mam! (*He clutches the rope of the swing in terror and howls*)

The Lights cross-fade to the general state

The two girls and Sam are standing in a group by the climbing frame and watching his antics

Wendy Do you think we should get him down?
Ellie I don't know if we can.

They go over and make attempts to pull him off the swing. He panics and clutches harder

Shurrup. Shurrup. You little sod.
Wendy Get him down.

Sam and the Baby are crying in sympathy. The two girls attempt to help Johnny down. In the process they all end in a heap on the floor in tears

Ellie Shurrup. Shurrup. Shurrup. (*She lays about her and knocks them all into silence*)
Johnny (*to the audience*) See what I mean?

The Lights cross-fade to the spot on the Baby's blanket. Johnny walks over to him

Baby (*playing with his feet and not looking at Johnny*) Was it worth it, then?
Johnny (*casually*) Oh, you mean the swing.
Baby Yes. Of course I mean the swing. Do you remember why you did it?
Johnny Well. I think so. Just about.

Baby And was it worth it?
Johnny Well… on balance…
Baby Yes. On balance.
Johnny On balance… I dunno.
Baby You see. That's the difference between you and me.
Johnny The difference?
Baby Yes. The difference is that I would know why I did it and
   whether it was worth it.
Johnny I see…
Baby And if it was me it would not be a tiddling old swing. It would
   be…

*The Lights cross-fade to the general state and the Baby looks behind
at the climbing frame. Johnny's eyes follow his*

Johnny Right. (*He grabs the Baby's blanket and pulls him over to
   the highest part of the frame*)

*The Baby falls over in the process, gurgling and laughing. Johnny
stands looking at the frame, puzzling out a solution. Sam realizes
what is happening and runs over*

Sam No! You can't do it. You musn't do it!
Johnny If you tell me he'll fall off, I'll poke your eyes out.
Sam He will. He'll fall off.

*Johnny attempts to poke Sam's eyes out, but is overwhelmed by
superior strength and is sat upon by Sam*

Johnny (*to Sam; darkly*) You wait till we're both the same age.
Wendy Get off him! (*She cuffs Sam and pulls him off*)
Ellie Get off him! (*She cuffs Wendy and pulls her off Sam*)

*Honour satisfied and the pecking order re-established, the two girls
go off to play by the swing*

Johnny Look. He really wants it. He wants to go to the top.

Sam He'll only f… He won't be able to stay up there. He'll hurt
  himself.
Johnny You were going to say…
Sam No, I wasn't. I jus' said he'll hurt himself.
Johnny And how will he hurt himself?
Sam He'll fall off.
Johnny (*triumphantly*) There. You said it.
Baby (*scornfully*) Has it occurred to you that you haven't achieved
  a great deal so far? May I suggest that Sam negotiates with
  Wendy. She hasn't quite had all the sense knocked out of her yet.
  After all, she is only seven.
Sam What did he say?
Johnny He said ask Wendy.
Sam But she'll tie me up with rope and pinch me.
Johnny So?

*Sam sighs and gingerly approaches the girls. Wendy has her back
to him. He tugs on her dress*

Sam Wendy?
Wendy (*through her teeth*) Go away!
Sam Wendy?
Wendy I said, go away. Go away!
Johnny He's not very good at this, is he?
Baby Oh, he'll be all right. There's an automatic mechanism that
  will set in any moment and get all the attention he needs.
Sam *Wendy?*
Wendy Go away! (*She turns and slaps him*)

He bursts into tears

Baby (*pleased*) Told you so.
Ellie Oh God!

Ellie stomps off L

Wendy Shurrup! Shurrup. Oh please shurrup. Oh… there, there.
  (*She places an arm around him in a perfunctory manner*)

He sidles out of it

    (*Experimentally*) Didums.
Baby Didums!? For goodness sake.
Wendy Waddamatter then?
Baby I think I'm going to throw up.
Wendy What can Wendy do, eh?
Sam (*sobbing gently*) It's the baby…
Wendy Well, let's have a look at him.

They go over and she examines the Baby inexpertly

Sam (*abruptly*) He wants to climb to the top of the frame.
Wendy (*aghast*) But he'll fall off.
Johnny I can't bear it.
Sam It's imp… imp… imp…
Johnny ⎫
Baby ⎭ (*together*) Important.
Wendy What did they say?
Sam (*sullenly*) Nuthin'.
Johnny If he gets it wrong, I'll kill him.
Baby He'll get it wrong.

The Lights cross-fade to the off-centre spot. Sam walks into it

Sam It is all very confusing. It starts off straightforward enough and gets complicated as it goes on. We have the most amazing filing system in our heads. It all cross-refers. Our senses take information and mesh it in. If we get hurt some way then blockages cause information to be distorted. If you fall over, the pain distorts things. If someone calls you a prat when you've done your best, it gives you a warped picture of yourself. Of course, you need feedback from the world; but some of it hurts like hell.

That's when the feelings set in.

And we have some wonderful ways of dealing with feelings.

There's nothing wrong with feelings. They are as natural as breathing; but you do have to do something about them. Watch when the baby gets hurt. He cries for a bit and then carries on as if nothing happened. The crying clears up the feelings caused by the pain. If he gets frightened, he laughs. If he's terrified, he shakes. Does the job nicely.

Of course, as you grow up, you have all that shaken out of you. Big boys don't cry. Girls mustn't show their anger. Yawning's good, all that oxygen to the brain in a quick shot to wake you up; but you mustn't do it; or you stop it with your hand. You can't even fart. So you spend the rest of your life worrying about indigestion.

Grim, isn't it? You get hurt for all the things you can do to relieve the pain you already have.

So the pain gets frozen in place and the wrong information builds up.

But right now I know that it is one way of getting unconditional attention. (*He begins to cry*)

The Lights cross-fade to the general state

Wendy Now there. Stop. Stop. Please stop. Go on.
Sam Baby.
Wendy We can't put him up there. Not safe. He'll only…
Sam ⎫
          ⎬ (*together*) Fall off.
Wendy ⎭
Johnny I'm not going to listen.
Baby It's all right. He's just about clinched it.

Sam looks into Wendy's eyes with a pleading, trembling lipped anguish. She has an idea and looks at the frame in a calculating fashion

Wendy I know. I can use my rope and tie him up there.

Johnny He's done it.

Baby No way. I am having nothing to do with her and that skipping rope. I've seen what they can do with it. She'll strangle me.

Wendy That's what we'll do. We just have to use our brains a bit. He'll never fall off.

Johnny You're going up there, old buddy.

Baby Not under any circumstances. She'll break my leg at the least. They'll never get me down. I'll starve to death. Tell her to put that bloody rope away.

Johnny Sam. Tell her not to use the rope.

Sam looks at the gleam in her eye

Sam I've as much chance of writing the *Encyclopaedia Britannica*.

Wendy Up you go, then.

The three begin to climb the frame, hanging the Baby from convenient places as they gain footholds

Johnny Sorry.

Baby Sorry. Sorry. What do you mean sorry?! Tell her to put that bloody rope away.

Wendy What's he crying for?

Sam Er… He's not crying. He's laughing.

Wendy Oh. Right.

Baby What's this—a conspiracy?!

Johnny Well, you wanted to go up, didn't you?

Baby Yes, I did. But not if it means hanging from the neck until dead at the end of it.

They have reached the top. Wendy straps the Baby's chest to a cross beam

Johnny That's not so bad, is it?

Baby (*grudgingly*) I suppose not. I might survive the rope burns and the vertigo.

The three help each other down and survey the result. Wendy is very pleased

Wendy I learnt that knot in the Brownies.
Johnny Congratulations. I suppose they'll teach you how to undo it next week.
Wendy What did he say?
Sam Nuthin'.
Wendy Well, he's stopped crying now.
Sam Probably dead.
Wendy What?
Sam Nuthin'.

She goes to hang on the swing

Johnny Are you frightened?
Baby No. No. I've got over that.
Johnny What's it like?
Baby Pretty good as it goes.
Johnny Can you remember?
Baby Why we did it? Yes. I'll remind you later.
Johnny What now?
Baby Oh, I'll just stop around here for a bit.
Sam What did he say?
Johnny He said he'd stay there for a bit.
Sam I don't think he's got much of a choice.
Baby What did he say?
Johnny Nuthin'.

The Lights cross-fade to the swing

Wendy I remember some things about when I was little. I remember twilight and the horses in the front room. I could reach up to two of them and swing; or climb on one and ride the universe. They were probably the chair arms on the suite; but they were horses then. And there were voices all around, sweet and loving but not quite distinguishable or understandable; I couldn't be sure if they were people.

I remember lying in the soft and warm, watching the light and laughing at things in front of me. I don't know what they were. They might have been my hands. They might have been people. They were talking or making noises. The light was so fresh.

Then something happened. I think it must have been school. Ritualised torment. I was terrified that first day, but I didn't know what of. The teacher asked who wanted dinner. I thought it was a good idea, so I put my hand up like lots of people did. I didn't have any money, so the teacher said it was OK and she would sort it out later. It took her a long time to cook it and she didn't do a lot. We just played a few games. Then we went into the hall and sat down. There were hundreds of us. I don't know where they all came from. And it was very noisy. Then just as I got my dinner, my mam came in. She looked very worried. She got my coat and put it on me and we left in a hurry. The children were all laughing, and the dinner ladies. Hundreds of them. Laughing at me.

I've been laughed at, and smacked and told off and confused ever since. And when it makes me angry I get smacked harder and sent to bed.

And no-one gets close. We hardly ever even hold hands with people any more. You get told off if you hug anybody but your mam and sometimes your dad. People mock you if you even touch a boy.

I'm lonely. And alone. (*She sits on the floor and quietly sobs*)

The Lights cross-fade to the blanket. Johnny and Sam are sitting holding hands

Johnny We did very well.

Sam Did we? Did we?

Johnny To get him up there.

Sam Wendy.

Johnny No. It was all of us. Baby told me, I told you and you …
    told Wendy. We all did it.

Sam Did we?

Johnny Do you know why now?

Sam Yes. Yes, I think so.

Johnny Good lad.

Sam Why's she crying.

Johnny She can't remember. Go get her.

*Sam goes gently to Wendy and takes her hand. He brings her to the
blanket where the three sit in a gentle hug until she stops crying. The
Lights cross-fade to the general state*

    (*Suddenly*) With a bit more help we could tell the adults!

Sam Tell them what?

Johnny What they're doing wrong; and how to put it right!

Baby You're cracking up.

Johnny We just have to do it in stages and pass the message on.

Baby You're out of your skull and through the other side.

Johnny They won't have to do much to change things, will they?

Baby Not a lot.

Johnny We can make the universe a zestful, loving, wonderful
    place.

Baby It'll never work.

Johnny So the next step is…

Ellie enters L

Sam (*seeing her*) Ellie.

Johnny Yes. Ellie.

Baby She'll kill the lot of you.

Ellie disdainfully ignores them and wanders to stand in front of the

*blanket. Johnny leaps at the back of her knees and she collapses
backwards onto the heap of children who allow her to fall on to the
blanket. Johnny lies on her legs*

Johnny Sit on her.
Sam What?
Johnny Sit on her. If we can get her attention long enough, we can
   tell her.
Baby Dream on, soldier.

*Sam sits on Ellie's chest, facing the audience. Seeing her chance,
Wendy straddles her shoulders and pins her arms. Ellie struggles
and makes appropriate noises*

Johnny Look as if you're going to cry and tell Wendy not to hit her.

Sam puts on the appropriate faces and tugs Wendy

Sam Don't hurt Ellie…

Wendy pokes Ellie. Sam bursts into tears

Wendy Don't tell Mam. Oh, stop. Stop. Shurrup.

Sam dutifully stops crying. Ellie continues to struggle and complain

Baby You won't be able to tell her anything while she's making that
   din.
Johnny What can we do about it?
Baby Well, what does everybody else do?
Johnny (*inspired*) Shurrup!
Sam (*enjoying himself*) Shurrup! Shurrup!
Wendy Shurrup!
All (*ad hoc*) Shurrup! Shurrup! Shurrup!

Ellie shuts up

Baby (*sarcastically*) Brilliant.

Johnny Now, Sam, listen carefully. Tell Wendy to tell Ellie that she doesn't have to go round slapping and pinching people.

Sam And pushing them over and stealing their ice-creams.

Baby And sitting on people.

Johnny Look, if you're not going to help, just shut up, will you?

Baby Help? I'm not even going to look. (*He closes his eyes tight to reinforce the point*)

Sam Wendy? Wendy? (*He tugs at her dress*)

Wendy What?

Sam She said, "What".

Johnny I figured out that much. Tell her. Go on, tell her.

Sam (*after a pause*) What have I got to tell her?

Baby She'll have died of starvation by the time you work it out.

Johnny (*wisely and kindly*) It's all right. Sammy, you'll remember.

Baby That's the stuff.

Johnny Thank you.

Sam Tell Ellie she doesn't have to hit anyone.

Wendy What?

Sam looks at Johnny

Johnny Yes. I heard.

Sam Tell her that she's just distorting reality and setting in distress that will rattle down the ages. Tell her to get close to people and cherish them and nurture the universe.

Johnny Very good.

Baby Excellent.

Wendy What?

Sam Go on. Tell her. You'll remember.

Baby I'm proud of you, son.

Wendy (*tentatively*) Don't hit me.

Johnny What?

Sam No!

Baby Oh, for God's sake!

Wendy Please, please, don't hit me. (*She cries*)

Johnny Jesus wept.
Baby And well he might.
Ellie Gerroff! Gerroff! Ya buggers!
Wendy Buggers?
Sam What's that mean?
Johnny Haven't a clue.
Baby You don't want to know.

Ellie starts to struggle and complain loudly

All Shurrup!

Ellie does

Baby I just wondered.
Johnny I hope this is useful.
Baby I just wondered how long you were going to keep this up for.
Johnny How long?
Baby Yes. The three of you are not exactly strong enough; and I
   doubt if you will get the message across this century. So how
   long?
Johnny How long?
Baby And I was curious as to what you thought she was going to
   do when you let her get up.
Johnny Get up. (*It is slowly dawning on him*)
Baby And what you would look like with a purple face, how long
   you will last without breathing, how long the bones would take
   to mend and that sort of thing.
Johnny Oh… Sammy.
Sam What?
Johnny When I say run, run.
Sam What?
Johnny This doesn't seem as good an idea as it was a moment ago.
   When I say run, run towards the adults over there and cry a bit.
Sam But she can outrun the lot of us and have a skip and a punch
   in between.

Johnny We've got to try, though. We'll have another shot at telling
  her later.
Sam You might, but I won't.
Johnny Run!
Wendy What?
Sam Run!

They get up and make to run off. Johnny falls over at once

  Wendy exits L in a hurry

*Ellie catches Sam, thumps and slaps him into sobbing and leaves
him on the blanket. She races after Wendy, brings her back and
bangs her head on the floor a few times. Then she thumps
Johnny's prone form and walks over him in satisfaction, then
goes off R*

The three lie sobbing

Baby (*with admiration*) Ruthlessly efficient. The Gestapo would
  have a lot to learn from her.
Johnny Shurrup.
Baby Touchy! Do you remember what you were telling her?
Johnny Erm… I don't know…
Baby Ask the others.
Johnny Sam. Do you remember?
Sam Remember…
Johnny Never mind. Ask Wendy.
Sam Wendy. Do you remember what we were saying?
Wendy What? Go away.
Baby Works every time.

The group gather their senses and prepare to play

  Wendy skips off

Johnny Is it still good up there?

Baby Oh, yes. You get a totally different perspective on things. And look. Just over there.

Johnny looks R

That tree is the highest in the park. Beautiful, isn't it? You can imagine it touching the heavens. What it would be to sit at the top of that, eh?

Johnny Yes. So high. So high. What a symbol. What an achievement.

Sam What?

Johnny (*taking his hand*) The tree. Look at that tree.

They wander off R *together, looking up, hand in hand*

Baby They never learn. One door shuts and another one closes. It's getting a bit chilly up here. My nappy is full of smelly, cold stuff. The rope hurts. It's a long way down.

Hey! You lot. I've had enough now. We did it, didn't we? It's time for my nap. Come back and get me down. I'm cold. I might fall off. I'm getting frightened. Come on, enough's enough. I could die up here. They'll find nothing but a few bones and a skipping rope. Hey! Hey! Oh, dear. Oh, dear. Help! Help! I want my mam.

Mama! Mama! Mama!

His cries are added to by the sound of a crying baby, which takes over and then fades out. The Lights cross-fade to the swing spot

Ellie walks into it with a dog-eared notebook and a pencil. She is concentrating hard

Ellie (*writing*) Dear dairy. Today I played in the park. I looked after the children. They were very, very naughty. Wendy would not let me skip and Johnny fell off the swing. Then they tied the baby to the climbing frame. He could of died. Later they sat on me so I gave them a good smacking.

Then Sam and Johnny tried to get up the big tree. They got very, very high and Johnny fell off. The nurse mended him with bandages and things.

I am a good girl. I am going to be a nurse or a teacher or an air hostess or something. I am going to help people to be good and tell them off when they are not. (*She signs with a flourish*) Ellie. Aged nine and a bit.

The Lights fade out and there is the sound of children playing as——

——the CURTAIN *falls*

FURNITURE AND PROPERTY LIST

On stage: Swing
Climbing frame
Rug

Off stage: Skipping rope (**Ellie**)
Baby's bottle (**Johnny**)
Five ice-creams (**Ellie** and **Wendy**)
Dog-eared notebook, pencil (**Ellie**)

LIGHTING PLOT

Property fittings required: nil
1 exterior. The same throughout

To open: Darkness

Cue 1	The sound of a baby crying *Spot on the area of the swing*	(Page 1)
Cue 2	**Ellie**: "…he can say is 'mama' and 'dada'." *Cross-fade to general lighting*	(Page 1)
Cue 3	**Sam** and **Johnny** exit *Cross-fade to a spot on the **Baby**'s blanket*	(Page 4)
Cue 4	**Baby**: "…in this heap of dribbling blubber?" *Cross-fade to general lighting*	(Page 5)
Cue 5	Everyone exits but the **Baby** and **Johnny** *Cross-fade to a spot on the swing*	(Page 9)
Cue 6	**Johnny** howls *Cross-fade to general lighting*	(Page 11)
Cue 7	**Johnny**: "See what I mean?" *Cross-fade to a spot on the **Baby**'s blanket*	• (Page 11)
Cue 8	**Baby**: "It would be…" *Cross-fade to general lighting*	(Page 12)

Cue 9	**Baby**: "He'll get it wrong."	(Page 14)
	Cross-fade to the off-centre spot	

Cue 10	**Sam** begins to cry	(Page 15)
	Cross-fade to general lighting	

Cue 11	**Johnny**: "Nuthin'."	(Page 17)
	Cross-fade to the swing	

Cue 12	**Wendy** sits on the floor and quietly sobs	(Page 18)
	Cross-fade to the blanket	

Cue 13	**Wendy** stops crying	(Page 19)
	Cross-fade to general lighting	

Cue 14	The sound of a crying baby fades out	(Page 24)
	Cross-fade to the swing spot	

Cue 15	**Ellie**: "Aged nine and a bit."	(Page 25)
	Fade lights out	

EFFECTS PLOT